In this story...

SUGAR - H̶
changes (
can make
she sings

BLAZE - My toy dragon. He snorts fire and he can fly but he is a bit scared of pretty much everything.

HANNAH - I've tried to draw her name to show you what she's like. She jumps into things and has lots of feelings and stuff.

JO - That's me! I'm just me really. But every time we have a magical adventure with Sugar and Blaze, I'm the one who writes it down.

THIS is our latest adventure...

The Sugar and Blaze Adventures

Have you read them all?

That's Rubbish! ☐ Tinselpants! ☐ Prince Charm-Bin! ☐

Nuts! ☐ Walk The Plank! ☐

WALK THE PLANK!

Jenny York

ILLUSTRATED BY LUKE COLLINS

For all the kids, in all the schools I've visited so far. It was GREAT to meet you!

Text copyright © Jenny York, 2024
Illustrations copyright © Luke Collins, 2024

The moral right of the author and illustrator has been asserted
All right reserved.
No part of this publication may be reproduced or transmitted or utilised in any form or by any means, electronic, mechanical, photocopying or otherwise without the prior permission of the publisher.

First published in Great Britain in 2024 by Saltaire Books, Bradford, England.

CHAPTER 1

We were on holiday at the seaside when the magic began again!

Me and my little sister Hannah had just been swimming in the sea with our Dad. We were walking back up the beach to find the others when Hannah said,

"Do you think there are any sharks around here?"

She didn't look scared. She looked excited. She probably thought she could fight a shark and win. Typical Hannah!

Dad looked excited too because he had spotted a chance to be silly.

Our Dad loves being silly!

"Sharks?" he whispered, pretending to look around in alarm. "Do you mean here on the beach, Hannah? Hiding somewhere in all these people?"

"Dad," I grinned. "She meant in the sea."

But Dad wasn't listening. He was busy enjoying himself with this new crazy idea.

"Oh Hannah," he gasped. "The sharks could be wearing disguises! WAIT! I think that's one over there!"

He pointed to a very, VERY old lady, asleep in a deckchair and we both giggled.

"Seriously though…" said Hannah after a few more steps. "COULD there be any sharks in the sea here?"

"Oh no! Far too cold!" said Dad, but

his eyes were still twinkling with silliness. "Truthfully, the only thing in this sea will be LOTS and LOTS of...**SEA DRAGONS!**"

"Da-ad," grinned Hannah, "There aren't any sea dragons."

"Yes there are!" insisted Dad. "In fact the next time we go swimming, **we should probably take Blaze to protect us!**"

Dad winked at me as if he was being totally hilarious and I grinned back.

But this time Dad was being less silly than he realised. Because Blaze REALLY CAN look after people!

I guess I should tell you about Blaze...

You see, Blaze isn't a SEA dragon. He's a TOY dragon.

MY toy dragon!

And before you say I'm too old for a fluffy blue dragon toy, there's something you should know!

Blaze was a gift from my Grandma and at the same time Hannah got this cuddly toy fairy called

Sugar.

Sounds normal so far, right?

WRONG!

Because no one else knows but these two toys...come to life!

Sugar becomes a colour-changing, constantly-singing nightmare that my sister adores...

and Blaze becomes a real dragon that can fly and breathe fire!

Even better, with the help of Sugar's magical dust, Blaze can grow as big as a car and carry us wherever we need to go.

And having a massive flying dragon comes in handy more often than you'd think...

Because since we got the toys, me

and Hannah sort of ATTRACT magical trouble.

Anyway, back to the story...

As the sand under our feet changed from wet to dry, I spotted our baby cousin Ruby.

She was playing with her new sand toys - three tiny moulds in the shape of a turtle, a crab and a dinosaur.

And next to her on the sand was Uncle Ed.

"You look freezing!" he laughed when he saw us. "Need some towels to warm up?"

"Towels might not be enough, Ed!" joked Dad as Uncle Ed handed them out. **"I think we might need ICE CREAMS!"**

"Da-ad!" grinned Hannah. "Ice creams don't warm you up!"

"Well, they warm ME up!" smiled Dad and everyone laughed.

Just then Mum came stomping over the sand towards us.

"Unbelievable!" she spluttered, looking SUPER mad. **"I was... I mean... A SEAGULL just attacked me!"**

"WHAT?" cried Dad. "What happened?"

"It flew right at me!" said Mum. "Flapping all round my head and squawking. I'd just got some ice creams." She pulled a face. "But that silly bird made me drop them."

"Despicable!" cried Dad. **"Seagulls are the EVIL SUPER VILLAINS of the seaside. I've always said so!"**

I grinned and Hannah giggled.

"But never mind about the ice creams," said Dad. **"Let's just go back and get ten more!"**

"TEN?" gasped Mum. "Why on earth do we need ten? There are only six of us!"

"Six people," agreed Dad. But then he started counting on his fingers, muttering silly made-up maths.

"So that's two each. Plus THREE for me... borrow something from the tens column (who knows why?) and...YES!" he grinned. **"We need THIRTEEN more!"**

"MORE MORE!" cried Ruby, looking up from her sand toys and clapping her hands in delight.

She's only two, so she doesn't really get jokes...or numbers even! But she's a BIG fan of MORE.

"We only need six!" said Mum firmly, but she was smiling with everyone else now. "And let's go and get them together this time," she decided. "Safety in numbers and all that!"

"Exactly!" cried Dad. "And the **bigger**

the number, the **safer** you are! Which is why we need thirteen ice creams! Fourteen might be safer still! **I don't mind eating an extra one,"** he beamed happily, **"if it's a matter of keeping people safe!"**

★★★

We headed up to the ice cream van and before long we were eating ice cream and strolling along the prom.

(Prom just means the path bit behind the beach. It's short for promenade. Uncle Ed told me that!)

Anyway, Uncle Ed was licking Ruby's ice cream to stop it running all over her fingers and I was looking out across the sea, trying to spot ships.

In the distance there was an old lighthouse, perched on the end of the cliffs. And a bit nearer to the shore...

"Hannah!" I frowned, grabbing her arm and pointing. "What's that?"

"What's what?" asked Hannah, turning to

look.

But at that moment a cloud passed in front of the sun...and suddenly I was pointing at nothing.

The SParkling Something, that I THOUGHT I'd seen out at sea...

...had VANISHED!
Or maybe I'd **just imagined it**?
And then,
"Arghhhhh!" cried Hannah,
waving her arms above her head.
"HEEEEEEELP!"

CHAPTER TWO

Flapping around Hannah's head was A HUGE SEAGULL!

"NOT AGAIN!" yelled Mum, dashing to help. **"CLEAR OFF YOU PESKY..!"**

At once the seagull swooped away. But as it did, it gave a screechy cry...that sounded a lot like laughter!

That's when I SHOULD have guessed. I should have spotted that another magical adventure was starting!

But, to be fair, it was the next morning before things went PROPERLY bONKERS...

Let me explain.

You see, Hannah and I had gone down to the beach with our Uncle Ed. Our plan was to go for an early morning swim but,

"The life guards haven't put the safety flags out yet!" said Uncle Ed crossly and then he turned to us. **"You two stay here while I go and sort this out."**

(Uncle Ed used to be a life guard himself when he was younger, so he loves telling other life guards what they're doing wrong.)

He **SPRINTED** off towards the Lifeguard Station and the second he was gone...

 Rustle Rustle Rustle

...the toys in our beach bags wriggled to life.

"Ahhhh, I love a good beach towel," sighed Blaze from inside my bag. "So snuggly and cozy! In fact, I think I'll have a little nap!"

"But, Blaze, you only just woke up!" giggled Hannah.

"Doesn't matter," Blaze mumbled drowsily. "You can't have too much sleep. It's good for you...like marshmallows!"

Hannah and I grinned but inside Hannah's bag, Sugar tutted.

"Well (unlike Mr Boring over there) I am ready for some ad-ven-ture!" she sang.

And with that she **BURST** out from the bag, **ZIPPED** above our heads, did a cheery loop-the-loop and started to sing,

"Oh, I do like to be beside the sea siiii- iii- iiiide!"

Luckily there was no one to see her. The beach was pretty much empty at this time in the morning!

But that didn't stop Blaze

13

worrying. **IN A FLASH** he came peeping out from under his towel, looking absolutely terrified.

"SUGAR!" he hissed. "Get back in that beach bag, right now! Someone will SEE you!"

"Oh, Blaaaaaze!" sang Sugar rolling her eyes. **"Don't be such a boring old bossy-bum!"**

Blaze looked between me and Hannah for help.

"Will someone please TELL HER!" he pleaded.

"Besides," sang Sugar merrily, **"if anyone DOES see me, they'll just think I'm one of those snee-gull thingies!"**

Blaze was really panicking now.

"It's SEA-gulls!" he spluttered. "Not Snee-gulls. **And SEA-gulls are WHITE, Sugar! Not purple, WHITE!"**

A very PURPLE Sugar blew a very RUDE raspberry...and then kept **WHIZZING** about enjoying herself.

"Or are they grey?" worried Blaze, peering up into the sky to check the colour of seagulls. "Oh, never mind! Just get back in the bag, Sugar!"

"Nooo-oo-oo waaaaay!" she sang and screwing up her face with effort...she turned herself white and grey.

Because that's something else you should know about Sugar!

She changes colour depending on how she's feeling. And if she tries really-really, very-very hard, she can even pick her own colours!

"There!" sang Sugar. **"Grey and white! Just like one of those snee-gull thingies. Happy now?"**

"Not really," flapped Blaze. "Because it's a SEA-gull not a Snee-gull. And unlike you they don't sing, Sugar! OR SPARKLE WITH FAIRY DUST!"

"Are you sure?" sang Sugar sweetly, pointing at a nearby bird. **"Because that one over there looks SUPER sparkly."**

She was right! One of the nearby seagulls did

look sort of SPARKLY in the sunshine... Which was odd!

It made me think about the SPARKLE I'd seen out at sea yesterday. Could THAT have been a seagull? But seagulls don't normally sparkle, do they?

It didn't make any sense!

"**Anyway never mind about sneeee-gulls!**" sang Sugar. "**Just looooook at all this MESS! You humans are SUCH a bunch of scruuuuuuff-buuuuums!**"

Hannah giggled at the 'scruff-bums' thing. But now she mentioned it, Sugar had a point!

Dotted around the sand, I could see plastic bottles and ice cream wrappers and forgotten beach toys.

I even spotted a half inflated flamingo swim ring! Maybe it had burst, or blown away, or something. But now it was sadly scuffing it's way down the beach in the wind!

It was a total mess!

Maybe people should get banned from the seaside if they didn't take their rubbish home with them!

I was about to say so when,

"Look out everyone!" called Hannah. "Uncle Ed's coming back with one of the lifeguards!"

"**Mmmmm, I just looooooove lifeguards!**" sighed Sugar, batting her eye lashes and turning golden-yellow with delight. "**Such haaaandsome helpeeeeeers!**"

"SUGAR!" snapped Blaze. "Stop with the yucky *love stuff* and GET BACK IN THE BAG!"

"And you might not looooooove this one, Sugar," added Hannah, peering down the beach. "This one looks all mean and grumpy."

"Uncle Ed looks cross too," I sighed. "I bet they've been arguing about the flags."

Hannah nodded. But just then,

a seagull screeched

over head and the lifeguard

FROZE like a statue!

Uncle Ed froze too! Then they both began

to SPARKLE in the sunshine.

It was as if they'd been hit by the beams from one of those disco glitter balls!

"Uh-oh!" whimpered Blaze. "That's bad! That's tummy twisty bad!"

"Magic!" whispered Hannah thoughtfully and,

"**Here we go agaaaaaaain!**" sang Sugar, sounding positively GLEEFUL about a new chance for us to be in danger!

That's when Uncle Ed and the lifeguard

unfROZE...and things went all kinds of crazy!

CHAPTER THREE

"This is my new BEST FRIEND!" screamed Uncle Ed, rushing over to us and pointing at the lifeguard. **"Let's all build sandcastles together!"**

"Whooppeeeee!" cried the lifeguard, clapping his hands in delight. **"I love sandcastles!"**

And they dropped down onto the sand and started to play.

"Errrrm, Uncle Ed?" said Hannah, carefully. "Are you...err...feeling okay?"

Uncle Ed didn't answer but,

"**Wait a chicken-tickling minute!**" cried the lifeguard, smacking his forehead. "**I can't just sit here playing sandcastles …**"

"...because you need to keep people safe?" finished Hannah, hopefully.

"**OH NO-NO-NO!**" chortled the lifeguard, as if that was a silly idea. "**The other lifeguards can do that. No! I can't play SANDCASTLES because I need to play …MERMAIDS!**"

And with that he scooped up a nearby clump of seaweed...and slopped it on to the top of his head with a

SPLAT!

Then he **SPRANG** to his feet and began to dance and sing!

"I am a merrrrrrrmaid! My hair is seeeea weed," he sang, twirling around. '**Sea-sea-sea, wee wee weeeeeeed!"**

Uncle Ed giggled and pointed at him.

"You just said **WEE WEE!**" he cried.

The lifeguard clapped his hand over his mouth. But then he grinned.

"I did!" he agreed cheekily. **"Wee wee!"**

That did it! They both fell against each other, laughing their heads off.

Sugar flew over to them and peered down at the lifeguard.

"Not Faaaaaair!" she pouted, turning blue. **"He's far too haaaandsome to be bonkers!"**

But then her eyes lit up with a new idea and she began to glow bright pink instead.

"Oh, I know, I know!" she sang. **"Maybe he just needs a** true love's kiiiiiiiiss! **To break a magical speeeeell."**

She puckered up her lips with delight but...

"SUGAR! NO!" shouted Blaze. **"Don't you DARE!"**

And that caused our NEXT problem because...

"Oh look! A fairy and a DRAGON!" cried the lifeguard, spotting the toys. **"NEW GAME! New game!** Let's bury the dragon in the sand."

"WAIT! WHAT?" squeaked Blaze but,

"No!" cried Uncle Ed grumpily, **"The dragon and me want to play your mermaid game."**

He pointed at the lifeguard's head.

"Give the dragon your pretty mermaid hair!"

"NO!" blurted Blaze waving his paws. "I mean...No thank you! **No pretty hair for me, thanks. I'm...err..."**

He looked around desperately for help.

"**He's allergic to hair!**" suggested Sugar grinning, "**and also fun!**" she added with a cheeky wink.

But Uncle Ed wasn't listening. He was moving towards the lifeguard, looking determined.

"**Give the dragon your hair!**" he demanded.

"**No! IT'S MINE!**" sulked the lifeguard. "**MINE! MINE! MINE!**"

He looked like he was about to throw a MASSIVE toddler tantrum. THEY BOTH DID!

Sugar pulled a face.

"You know, on second thoughts, lifeguards are not really my thiiiing!" she decided. **"But if we need to break a magical spell...maybe BLAZE could kiss him."**

"ME!" cried Blaze. "I'm not doing it! It was your yucky idea, Sugar! **YOU do it!"**

"Well, somebody needs to do SOMETHING!" snapped Hannah.

"Fine! Fine! Out of my way!" sang Sugar. **"We all know I'm the smart one here. I'll fix iiiiiit!"**

"Sugar," began Hannah, "Maybe don't..."

But it was too late.

Sugar **ZIPPED** over to the lifeguard, scooped up the sloppy seaweed hair and plopped it on to Uncle Ed's head...

Which DEFINITELY didn't fix ANYTHING!

Suddenly the lifeguard was chasing Uncle Ed screaming,

"Gimmee back my hair!"

And Sugar was chasing the lifeguard singing,

"Come here so I can kiss you, Mr. Bonkers!"

And Blaze was chasing Sugar yelling,

"Noooooooo!"

And Hannah was chasing Blaze shouting,

"Just...Don't...Wait..."

And I was pretty sure I should be chasing someone too!

But before I could decide who to go for, Uncle Ed yelled,

"STOP!"

And he stopped! Which of course made everyone bump into him. But it did at least calm things down a bit!

Uncle Ed seemed to be thinking hard, which I hoped was a good sign.

"What on earth are we DOING?" he asked, frowning around at everyone. **"This is all wrong!"**

Sugar looked hopefully between him and the lifeguard.

"Has it stopped?" I whispered. "The magic... Has it..?"

Hannah took a step towards Uncle Ed to check. But Blaze held up a paw, warning her to wait.

And it was a good job he did! Because just then, Uncle Ed's face cracked into a smile.

"Why waste time fighting," he grinned, **"when we could WALK THE PLANK?"**

"Walk the whaaaaat?" sang Sugar, but,

"Great idea!" cried the lifeguard, looking even more bonkers than before. **"Let's go and WALK THE PLANK!"**

And just like that, they both **SPRINTED OFF** towards the sea!

"WAIT!" called Hannah, panicking and looking around. "What plank? There isn't any plank!"

But then we saw it!

Not a plank! But something SPARKLY...and a flash of white and grey.

It was disappearing behind the Lifeguard Station.

"That's the baddy!" cried Hannah, pointing. "That's the sparkly villain that's sending everyone silly. Come on!"

And with no plan at all (typical Hannah) she **DASHED AWAY**...towards what was almost certainly a **MAGICAL MONSTER.**

So Hannah was running one way and Uncle Ed was running the other way!

But I could only help one of them!

"Always TOWARDS the danger," grumbled Blaze as we all **SPED** after Hannah. "I really need to get myself some safer friends."

"**Nonseeeeeense!**" sang Sugar as she **ZIPPED** along by his side. "**We are**

FAAAAAABULOUS!"

"And what about Uncle Ed?" worried Blaze. "And that other nutter who wanted to bury me in the sand? Will they be alright?"

"One's a lifeguard and the other's an ex lifeguard," sang Sugar. **"They'll be fine in the sea for a bit while we fix this!"**

That sort of made sense. I hoped she was right...

Meanwhile Hannah had reached the back corner of the Lifeguard Station and was waving for us to hurry up.

"Ready?" she hissed as I tiptoed to join her.

I nodded, Sugar gave a cheery thumbs up... and Blaze frantically shook his head.

But we couldn't just stand there forever!

So, holding our breath,

WE PEEKED BEHIND THE SHACK!

CHAPTER FOUR

There in the gloom, tucked between the sand dunes and the Lifeguard Station was...

ABSOLUTELY NOTHING!

Or almost nothing. The only thing there was a stinky, overflowing bin!

"That's RUBBISH!" pointed out a nearby Caterpillar, (before remembering that he was from a different Sugar and Blaze story and should probably get back).

Anyway, the point is, there was no sparkling super-villain in sight!

"Nothing here!" admitted Hannah, and a

little frown crumpled her forehead.

But then the bin began to wobble and rustle and out popped...

a SEagull!

"Good grief!" cried the seagull and a half-eaten burger dropped from his beak. "Who d'you fink you are, sneakin' up on a bird like that?"

"Never mind who WE are!" snapped Hannah. "Who exactly are YOU?"

"And also what are you doing with that biiiiiiiiiiin?" asked Sugar nervously.

She was stressing out BIG TIME because she's had some bad experiences with bins in the past.

The seagull landed on the sand and grinned.

"'Name's Sneagle!" he said. "Sneagle d'Seagull!"

And then he ripped a massive peck out of the half eaten bin-burger at his feet.

"An as for the bin bit," he mumbled with his mouth full. "Well, it's obvious, innit? I'm one of them there eco-warriors!"

"**Aha! I knew iiiiit!**" sang Sugar. "**The magic's sent this one loopy tooooooo! Loopy as an old granny's handwriting!**"

"HAM white-in?" spluttered Sneagle through his latest beak-full of burger. "That sounds TASTY! Can you eat a HAM white-in?"

"She said 'handwriting'," explained Hannah. "And, no! Handwriting is just marks on a bit of paper."

"Mmmmmm, that sounds tasty n'all," said Sneagle brightly. "Can you eat paper? Or that other thing...GRANNIES! Can you eat Grannies?"

"**Eat Grannies?**" giggled Sugar. "**Who are you? The Big Bad Wooooolf?**"

....and what a big <u>beak</u> you have Granny

"Okay, okay! Let's rewind a sec!" I suggested. "What do you mean by 'eco-warrior', Sneagle?"

He beamed at me, as if someone had FINALLY asked a decent question.

"Well, let me explain," he said. "Did you know that every year YOU HUMANS throw away millions of tons of food?"

"Yes!" said Hannah sadly. "I learned about it at school. It's dreadful for the environment!"

(Hannah LOVES the environment. She even goes to a club about it at lunchtimes.)

"Exactly!" agreed Sneagle pointing his wing at Hannah and nodding. "So I'm back, 'ere, in this bin, savin' the planet." He winked at us. "One greasy, half-eaten burger at a time!"

"Er, just one thought on thaaaat!" sang Sugar pulling a face. "Yu-uuuuuuuck!"

Sneagle's eyes sparkled.

"Mmmm! Yu- uuuuuuuck sounds tasty n'all!" he said, excitedly. "Can you eat yu-uuuuuuuck?"

"You already are eating yuck," muttered Blaze, looking like he might be sick.

Hannah frowned.

"I don't think Sneagle is the evil super villain we're looking for," she admitted.

"Four?" echoed Sneagle, turning his full

attention to Hannah. "Four what? And can I have five, maybe? 'Cos I'm a bit peckish! GET IT? Peckish!" he laughed. "Because I'm a bird! Peck, peck!"

Blaze rolled his eyes and Sugar giggled.

But Hannah had made a good point! Sneagle wasn't the magical baddy!

So who was?

"Look, Sneagle," I tried. "You haven't seen anyone acting weird lately, have you?"

"Weirder than yooooooou," added Sugar sweetly, as if that was helpful. And not rude.

Sneagle thought about this, scratching his head with his wing.

"As a matter of fact," he said eventually, "things are a bit funny up at the ice cream van! Come on! I'll show you!"

Now you're probably thinking that Sneagle just fancied an ice cream. A nice BIN ice cream for pudding after his BIN burger. That's TOTALLY what I was thinking.

But I was WRONG!

Because when we got there...

"Does that count as odd?" asked Sneagle pointing his wing.

It really did!

The man in the van was TWIRLING on the spot, wiggling his arms and jiggling his legs.

"Hell-ooooooooo!" he waved, when he spotted us. "I'm an octopus!"

"Funny sort of octopus," pointed out Sugar. **"You've only got four tentacles!"**

The man frowned. Then he did a quick count of his arms and legs and...

"Oh, you're right!" he wailed, clutching at his face. **"How embarrassing. But hold on though...I can fix it!"**

He sprang to his ice cream machine and began to pump a huge swirl into his biggest type of cone. Then, with a mad look in his eye, he splatted the whole thing...

SQUELCH!

...right onto his jumper!

"There!" he beamed, pointing proudly at the cone. **"That makes FIVE tentacles! Three more to go!"**

He snatched up a second cone. But as he did, the first ice cream came unstuck and dropped to the floor with a messy

SHLOP!

"Yippee!" yelled Sneagle and he swooped forward to gobble it up but,

"No! Shooo!" shouted the man wafting him away. **"That's my TENTACLE! I need it! I'm an octopus I tell you! An ICE CREAM OCTOPUS!"**

"Hold on! Hold on!" sang Sugar. **"I've**

had another one of my perfect ideas!"

And flying into the van she scooped up the ice cream from the floor.

Then, with a cheeky wink...she squelched it

SPLAT!

right onto the man's head!

"There!" she grinned. **"Now you can be an ice cream UNICORN instead!"**

"SUGAR!" gasped Blaze in horror but,

"Brilliant!" cried the man as little rivers of ice cream started to run down his forehead. **"I'm a UNICORN! Neigh Neeighhhh!"**

"Told you it was odd!" grinned Sneagle.

"Bonkers," agreed Hannah, as the man started to snort and gallop about in his van, "But I don't think THIS is our magical baddy either!"

And then, as if to prove her point, the man screamed,

"Neighhhhhhhhhhhhh! I'm off to **WALK THE PLANK!"**

CHAPTER FIVE

"**Oh no you don't!**" cried Sugar and QUICK AS A FLASH she sprinkled the ice cream man with her magical dust.

At once, he shrank to the size of a teeny tiny mouse!

"Neeeeigh!" he squeaked, peering up at us from the floor of his van and shaking his tiny fist. "I'm still a unicorn! And I'm still going to WALK THE PLANK."

"**Of course you are!**" sang Sugar.

Then she flicked his sign to 'CLOSED' and slid the van window shut.

"**Voila!**" she grinned. "**Problem solved!**"

"I guess," worried Hannah, pulling a face. "But now what do we do?"

"I know!" cried Sneagle. 'Look at that!"

It was a boy and his Mum walking along the prom. They were each nibbling a breakfasty treat from a paper bag. And the boy was talking excitedly with his mouth full.

"**...but I DID see one mum!**" he insisted. "**An' it could talk, an' it had a pirate eye patch (but a sparkly one), an' it was down by the rock pools.**"

"Oh, Archie," laughed his Mum, shaking her head as they passed, "you've got such an imagination..."

Hannah grabbed my arm.

"Are you thinking what I'm thinking?" she whispered.

"That depends," said Sneagle. "Are YOU thinking that we should chase that boy an' nick his breakfast?"

"No," sighed Blaze. "She's thinking that there's some sort of magical monster down in the rock pools!"

Hannah nodded.

"And whatever it is," she added, "I bet it's got a sparkly pirate eye patch! Come on!"

And off we went again, chasing after her.

The rock pools were at the very end of the beach (almost where the cliffs began) and when it was high tide the sea sloshed into them, filling them with tiny creatures.

"One question!" asked Sneagle, flying along beside us as we RACED over the sand towards the rocks. "Can you EAT an eyepatch?"

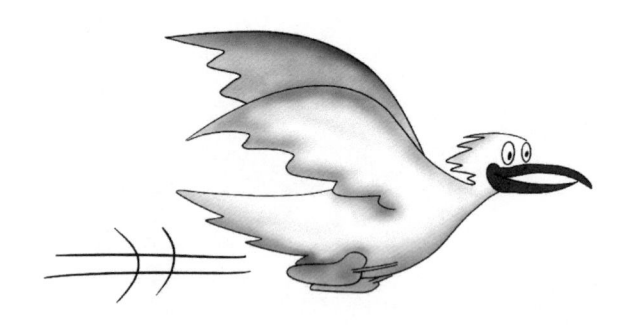

Sugar giggled but Blaze had clearly had enough.

"Sneagle," he said, in his EXTRA polite voice. "Why not get back to your burger. This could be dangerous!"

"He's riiiiight!" agreed Sugar, turning silver with excitement. **"When we have adventures, there's always LOTS of**

danger!"

"Oh, that's nice!" grinned Sneagle. "I'm a big fan of LOTS. A BIG BIG fan! Now does this danger come with anything? Maybe some chips or..."

"Everyone, please just...shhhh!" pleaded Hannah.

Because the rock pools were right ahead of us now!

We began to sneak and climb forwards. Over the small rocks. Around the bigger ones. Always doing our best to stay low and hidden. Always listening!

At first the only sound was the steady CRASH and SHHRRRR of the waves.

But then...

"So we do it tonight!" hissed an evil voice. **"At midnight tonight every stinking kid in this stinking holiday town...will WALK THE PLANK!"**

45

We all froze.

This was it! We'd found the baddy!

"And the ickle bitty CHILDREN can't swim!" sneered the cruel voice. **"They'll walk RIGHT to the bottom of the sea...and we will HAVE OUR REVEEEEEENGE!"**

Next to me Sugar gasped in horror and Blaze went pale. But Hannah looked fierce. Then she started edging forwards again.

She was going to take a peek!

I gulped, but Hannah was right. We had to look! We had to know!

As sneakily as we could, we all crawled to join her.

Hannah squeezed my hand. It was our secret signal. It meant 'Get Ready!'

I nodded.

And then...

together...

we peeked.

(Which means this is your moment to guess the magical baddy? Go on! Have a guess! You'll never get it!)

CHAPTER SIX

Floating in the middle of the nearest rock pool was...an **inflatable flamingo!**

In fact I was pretty sure it was the same flamingo as the one we'd seen yesterday. The one blowing down the beach.

Except now it was **ALIVE** and (you guessed it) wearing an eye patch!

And not just any old eye patch!

The whole thing was covered with blue and green gems that sparkled in the sunlight.

"So, what do you think to my plan?" asked the flamingo, and for a horrible second I thought it was talking to us.

I thought we'd been spotted! But that wasn't it.

At the edge of the rock pool there was a bucket and spade...and they were alive too!

Great! A magical villain with an evil gang. That was just what we needed!

Maybe you're wondering 'How evil can a bucket and spade really be?' Turns out – not very!

"Well, that sounds like a lovely plan, Doris!" said the spade cheerfully.

"Spade!" snapped the flamingo. **"How many times do I have to tell you? My NEW name is Pirate Pink!"**

"Oh, I'm DREADFUL with names!" chuckled Spade. "Can't I just keep calling you Doris, Doris?"

"Why would you call her **Doris-Doris**?" giggled the bucket. "That'd be like calling me **Bucket-Bucket**."

"Oh, you are a funny one!" laughed Spade. "Bucket-Bucket...and Doris-Doris!"

And they both fell about laughing at that.

"ENOUGH!" screamed Pirate Pink. **"Just bring me the turtle toy!"**

"Righto, Doris Pirate Pink, Ma'am!" grinned Spade. "You're the boss!"

"The Boss-Boss!" sniggered Bucket, and Pirate Pink gave a deep sigh.

Bucket and Spade began to shuffle towards the edge of the rock pool, pushing something in front of them.

It was a tiny sand mould in the shape of a turtle. I guessed some kid must have lost it on the beach.

But, unlike Bucket and Spade, this bit of beach litter wasn't alive.

At least NOT YET!

"Behold my POWER!" screamed Pirate Pink and she titled back her head.

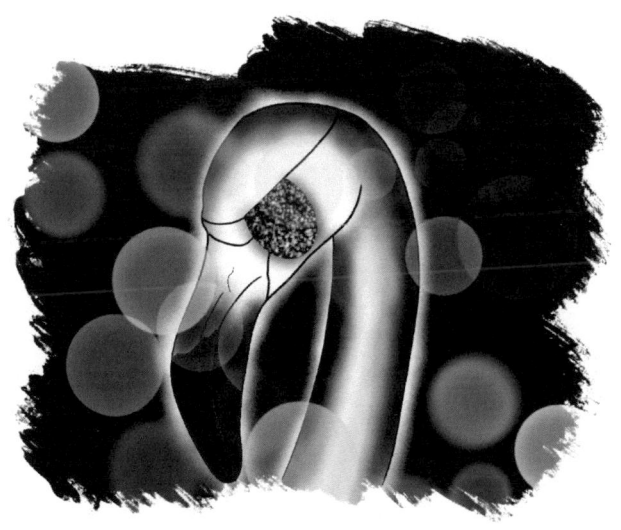

At once the sun hit the gems of her eye patch

and dots of light began to dance all around.

Just like the spots from a disco glitter ball!

Just like the SPARKLES we'd seen on Uncle Ed and the lifeguard!

Just like that SPARKLE I'd seen out at sea!

Things were finally starting to make sense!

As the dots of light danced, the tiny turtle began to sparkle too. Then it gave a little shiver.

And then...it opened its eyes.

It was alive!

Pirate Pink gave a crazed cackle.

"YA-KA-KA-KAAAAA!" she cried, throwing her pink wings wide in delight.

But then she pointed at the turtle and her expression became stern.

"ALIVE! And MINE to COMMAND!" she hissed. **"I name you...Tiny!"**

I felt a sharp tug on my arm as Hannah pulled me back down behind the rocks.

"So the eye patch is magical," she said breathlessly and everyone nodded.

"And that sparkly light is what sent Uncle Ed bonkers!" she added, grimly.

Lots more nods.

"Can you eat..?" began Sneagle but Sugar quickly clamped his beak shut.

Meanwhile my brain was starting to fizz and splutter with ideas.

"I bet that's what I saw out at sea," I whispered. "The eye patch!"

Hannah gasped.

"Maybe it floated in to the beach and brought the flamingo to life!"

Blaze nodded looking terrified.

"But now she's WEARING the eyepatch," he squeaked. "And using it to make herself a gang from the beach litter...Oh this is bad! Very, very bad!"

"Come on!" hissed Hannah. "We have to see what's going on!"

As quietly as we could, we all peeked again.

Down by the rock pool, Tiny the turtle was blinking and looking around.

"Whersies am I?" whispered Tiny. "Whersies my Ruby?"

Ruby?

My stomach did a weird flip...Surely she couldn't mean OUR Ruby?

But with a sinking feeling I realised our little cousin Ruby DID have a sand toy just like that turtle! She'd been playing with it on the beach.

Meanwhile, Pirate Pink was looking furious.

"Your STUPID little Ruby left you on the beach!" she snapped. **"Those careless little brats LEFT US ALL ON THE BEACH!"**

At first, Tiny looked frightened at this news. But then,

"It will be okay!" she decided and she put on a brave smile. "I tink my Ruby will be backsies for mees soon!"

"NO SHE WON'T!" screamed Pirate Pink. **"SHE LEFT YOU! You're one of us now!"**

Spade nodded furiously and Bucket winked saying,

"Welcome to the Doris-Doris gang, Tiny-Tiny!"

Luckily, Pirate Pink didn't hear because she was getting more and more angry by the second!

"And we will have our REVENGE!" she screeched. **"At MIDNIGHT tonight, the light from this eye patch will fall on the children's houses as they sleep. And every last stinking kid will want to WALK THE PLANK! Right into the SEA!"**

Tiny gave a horrified squeak.

"The sea!" gasped Tiny in horror. "The childrensies will be in d' sea? With-outa their grown-ups?"

Pirate Pink nodded gleefully. Spade, though, was looking a bit puzzled.

"Hold on, Pirate Doris Pink Ma'am!" he frowned. "How does light shine on your eye patch at midnight? Won't it be DARK at Midnight?

"**It will,**" she agreed. "**That's why we're going to use...**

THE LIGHTHOUSE!"

She pointed her wing at the tower in the distance and then, delighted at her own cunning, Pirate Pink began to laugh.

"**YA-KA-KA-KA!**" she cackled, her head rolling in circles on her long pink neck. "**YA-KA-KA-KAAAAA!**"

The eye patch sparkled brilliantly and dots of light began to spin about madly in every direction.

And this time it was dazzling!

I ducked away, shading my eyes.

But then I started to feel very, VERY, <u>VERY</u> hot.

And I realised something! I knew exactly how to cool off...It was so obvious...

I needed to go in the sea...

I needed to **WALK THE PLANK!**

CHAPTER SEVEN

As I **SPLASHED** into the sea, I realised that Hannah was right next to me. Sneagle and the toys were there too, flying above us and looking strangely alarmed.

"**Where are you two going?**" sang Sugar, who was flashing bright orange like a traffic light.

"I'm just going to **WALK THE PLANK**," called Hannah cheerfully. "Which reminds me... Does anyone have a pirate ship? With a plank?"

Now THAT was a very good point! **I didn't have a pirate ship!** And it looked like Hannah didn't have one either. **How annoying!**

"Let's just swim out to sea until we find one!" I suggested and Hannah nodded.

This felt like the smartest idea we'd had in ages.

"Errr, what about this!" cried Blaze looking frantic. **"I'll be your pirate ship! I can be a GREAT pirate ship! Sugar, DUST ME!"**

Sugar had turned ice blue, which didn't make any sense at all **because that's her absolutely terrified colour!**

Anyway, she sprinkled Blaze with her magical dust and immediately he grew to the size of a small boat. Then he flopped backwards into the waves, with his bright green tummy to the sky.

Hannah and I were already neck deep in the water.

"Perfect!" screamed Sugar. **"All aboard the lovely pirate ship!"** And she tugged at

place.

"You haven't got a pirate flag!" I pointed out.

"And if this is a pirate ship, where's the plank?" asked Hannah, looking around Blaze's tummy. "I want to **WALK THE PLANK!**"

"**Well, you can use Blaze's tail for a plank!**" suggested Sugar quickly.

"Tail to **WALK THE PLANK**," murmured Hannah nodding and trying to stand up.

"**But! NOT! YET!**" panted Sugar, tugging at Hannah to make her sit back down. "**Let's... errrrr...get a bit deeper first.**"

She gave Blaze a meaningful look and he nodded.

Immediately he went **ZIPPING OFF** like

59

a speed boat over the waves with Sneagle ~~SWOOPING~~ and ~~SOARING~~ above us.

Something didn't feel right. I wanted to get back in the water.

But as the beach became a blurry brownish line in the distance, the sea began to look colder... and darker...until at last, Hannah said,

"W-what...what just happened?"

She was shaking her head and frowning as if she'd just woken up from a nightmare.

I felt a lot like that myself!

Blaze slowed to a stop in the water.

"Well..." he began.

"You went bonkers and tried to chuck yourself in the seeeeeea," sang Sugar bluntly. **"Both of you!"**

"It was that flamingo," sighed Blaze. "Pirate Pink! She's got a very powerful magical object."

"The eyepatch!" I said, remembering.

Blaze nodded.

"And she's going to hurt the children!" remembered Hannah. "We have to get back there and stop her!"

Blaze nodded again.

"We do," he agreed. "But first we need a magical object of our own! Something more powerful than that horrible eyepatch!"

"Which means it's time for a magical adventuuuuure!" sang Sugar happily.

"Exactly!" agreed Blaze looking half-frightened and half-determined. "And luckily I know EXACTLY who we need to visit to get this all sorted out!"

"Really?" I asked. "Who is it? Is it someone sea-side-y?"

"A magical mermaid?" guessed Hannah.

"Oh please, pleeeeeease let it be a magical lifeguard," wished Sugar crossing all her fingers. **"A handsome ooooone!"**

Blaze pulled a face.

"Number one, Sugar - YUCK!" he said. "And number two – NO! We need to visit...the Pirate King."

"Sounds tasty!" cried Sneagle, swooping to land at my feet. "Can you eat a Pie-Rat? And shouldn't it be called a Rat Pie?"

"**Am-aaaaaaaa-zing!**" sang Sugar ignoring him. "**Pirates are even more dishy than liiiiiiifeguards.**"

"Don't worry 'bout a dish for me!" grinned Sneagle. "I'm 'appy eatin' my Pie-Rat off the floor!"

"**A Pirate kiiiing!**" sang Sugar dreamily, STILL ignoring him. "**Ohhhh and maybe I could be his Pirate Queeeeeeen!**"

She peered forward eagerly.

"**Let's get going, Blaze,**" she sang. "**And this time put your head right back in the water. That should speed things up!**"

"I don't want to get water in my eyes," grumbled Blaze. "And besides..."

But before he could finish, he made a sudden jerk in the water. Then another.

Then he started splashing and thrashing around!

"**Help!**" he squeaked, clutching at the air above him. "**HEEEEEEELP!**"

"Blaze!" gasped Hannah. "What's wrong? What's..?"

"**It's got my wings!**" he cried. "**It's pulling me under!**"

"What has?" screamed Hannah and together we scrambled across his tummy and grabbed his paws, trying to pull him up. But it was no use. Water was sloshing all around us!

Blaze was sinking!

"**Sugar, protect the children!**"

yelled Blaze. **"Use magic. Fly them out of here!"**

"Yes!" sang Sugar but,

"No!" I shouted gripping his paw even tighter. "We stick together. No matter what!"

And there wasn't time to argue!

Because at that moment Blaze was tugged under the water...

...AND THE DARK SEA SWALLOWED US UP!

CHAPTER EIGHT

Well, let's start with the good news, shall we?

As we sank into the sea, Sugar and Sneagle dive bombed after us and Sugar sprinkled us ALL with magical dust.

Now I've **no idea** how that stuff works but all at once we could SEE, HEAR and (best of all) BREATHE under water!

Amazing, right?

But then there was the BAD NEWS!

You see it turned out that we were completely and utterly surrounded by...

"Sea dragons!" squeaked Blaze.

There were maybe 30 of them! All the size of crocodiles with grey-blue scales and razor sharp fangs.

And the biggest one was swimming towards us!

"I AM WHARLA," he boomed, "KING OF THE SEA DRAGONS."

And then he turned to Blaze looking serious.

"NOW MOVE AWAY FROM YOUR EVIL KIDNAPPERS, YOUNG DRAGON-ME-LAD...SO THAT WE MAY KILL THEM!"

"**Errrr, what now?**" sang Sugar and,

"**Kidnappers?**" squeaked Blaze, his eyes wide. "This lot? Oh no...they're not kidnappers, Your, er, Highness. These are my **friends!**"

Wharla frowned.

"FRIENDS?" he growled. "THEN WHY HAD THEY DRAGGED YOU UP TO THE DANGERS OF THE SURFACE?"

"**Oh I seeeee!**" sang Sugar. "**You thought we were pulling Blaze OUT of the water!**"

"YOU WERE!" snapped Wharla crossly.

"**Only because you were pulling**

him IN to the water," sang Sugar sweetly. **"Before that we were just using hiiiiim as a booooat."**

Wharla looked outraged.

"USING HIM AS A BOAT?" he spluttered.

"Er n-no! Well...s-sort of," stammered Blaze. "But I was happy being their boat!" he added quickly. "Very, very happy!"

Some of the dragons gasped at this and a quite a few shook their heads in disgust.

"I SEE," said Wharla coldly.

He turned to the other dragons looking slightly embarrassed and muttered,

"IT WOULD SEEM THIS IS NOT A NOBLE AND FREE SEA DRAGON IN DISTRESS. 'TIS BUT A LAND DRAGON, SERVING ITS HUMAN MASTERS!"

He almost spat the 'land dragon' bit but then he shrugged.

"OUR WORK HERE IS DONE!"

At once, the other dragons began to drift away, rolling their eyes and muttering things like *'Unbelievable!'* and *'I was half way through a cup of tea, you know!'* but...

"Wait!" cried Hannah and the dragons stopped. "What exactly IS your work?"

Wharla turned back to Hannah, looking astonished that she didn't already know. But then he drew himself up, tall and proud.

"WE SEA DRAGONS GUARD THE OCEANS!" he boomed. "WE KEEP ORDER, RESCUE THOSE IN DISTRESS AND..." his eyes narrowed, "...CHASE OFF ANY OF THOSE NAUGHTY SHARKS THAT COME NOSING ABOUT!"

"**Sh-sh-sharks!**" stammered Blaze looking terrified.

"YES SHARKS!" nodded Wharla. "THINK THEY OWN THE PLACE AND..."

"**N-n-no!**" interrupted Blaze, panicking

and pointing. "I mean, **SH-SH-SHARKS!** Over there!"

We **SPUN** to look and Blaze was right!

In the distance a group of pale grey shapes were lazily stalking towards us.

In a flash, Wharla threw back his head and let out a howl like a wolf.

OW-WHOOOO

And then the howl seemed to echo around us as all the other dragons picked up the cry.

OW-WHOOOO

OW-WOOOOOOOO

"ATTACK!" boomed Wharla and at once all the dragons **SHOT AWAY** through the dark water.

I hoped their underwater eye sight was

better than mine because it looked to me like the sharks had already scarpered.

We were alone!

"Well, that was..." began Hannah but Blaze was shaking and pointing again.

"M-m-more sh-sh-sharks!" he stammered. "There's another pack, or shoal, or **whatever it is!**"

"Maybe it's a shimmy of sharks," sang Sugar and she did a little shimmy dance.

"Who cares!" squeaked Blaze. **"It won't matter what they're called if we've all been eaten by one!"**

(I found out later from Uncle Ed that it's called a SHIVER of sharks, which is pretty weird).

But Blaze had a point!

This new shiver of sharks was a lot further away. But now we had no sea dragons to protect us!

We needed to get out of the sea, AND FAST! There was just one problem...

Sugar had started a gentle doggie

paddle...towards the sharks!

"I'll take care of thiiiiis!" she smiled. "I'll just go siiiiiiiiiing at them!"

"Sugar!" squeaked Hannah. "This is no time for a concert!"

Sugar giggled.

"Of course not!" she agreed. "What I MEAN is that my singing will scare them awaaaaaaay."

"You're not that bad!" gulped Blaze.

"I'm not bad at all!" sang Sugar. "I'm brilliant. But I'm also LOUD! And sharks hate loud noiseeeeeees."

"WHAT?" shrieked Hannah.

"She's thinking of guinea pigs!" gasped Blaze, turning pale. "Sugar, it's **GUINEA PIGS** that are scared of loud noises!"

"No, Blaze," sang Sugar. "It's definitely sharks. I read about it in a library book."

"Sugar, seriously!" squeaked Blaze

starting to paddle after her. "That was Hannah's library book about **guinea pigs!"**

But Sugar wasn't listening.

"Sharkies! Sharkies! La-la-laaaa!" she screeched, waving at them.

"Does anyone have a snack?" gulped Sneagle. "Because being about to be eaten by sharks makes me hungry."

"Everything makes you hungry!" snapped Hannah, "Sugar, come back right now! We have to get out of here!"

I didn't say anything. I **was much too busy watching the sharks!**

You could see by the way these ones were moving that they hadn't spotted us yet...**but it was only a matter of time!**

"Sugar listen," tried Blaze. "Did this book **ALSO** say that **SHARKS LOVE CABBAGE** and make **GREAT FIRST PETS for children?**"

Sugar paused, looking thoughtful.

"Do you know what, Blaze, I think it did because..."

Suddenly her eyes went very wide.

"Oh crikey!" she sang, turning bright orange in alarm. **"I think it MIGHT have been a book about guinea pigs!"**

"EXACTLY!" agreed Blaze nodding furiously. "Guinea pigs! So let's all get out of here before..."

But it was too late.

"They've seen us!" squawked Sneagle flapping his wings in a mad panic and pointing at the sharks. "They're COMING!"

CHAPTER NINE

"**Everyone on my back! QUICK!**" cried Blaze.

But then a lot of things happened all at once!

First, Sneagle panicked and took a big, greedy, terrified bite into the nearest thing he could find...which was Blaze's tail.

SNAP!

Then, with an ear-splitting howl of

"ARRRRRRRR!"

Blaze began thrashing about, trying to shake

Sneagle off.

And last, but definitely not least...

THE SHARKS ATTACKED!

I grabbed Hannah, desperate to keep her safe. But actually, I needn't have worried. Because it turned out something **totally insane** was happening.

SWISH BONK!

Blaze was whipping and flicking his tail in every direction...

SWISH BASH!

He was desperately trying to shake off Sneagle!

SWISH POW!

But as he thrashed about..he was whacking into all the sharks!

SMASH! went the first one, flying off into the distance and **CRASH!** went the next one, spinning away sideways! It was like a bizarre game of rounders...where Blaze was the batter and every shark was just a new shiny ball to be whacked away with a **WHALLOP!**

And then...

AW-WOOOOOO!

The sea dragons were back! **SHOOTING** into the fight! Snapping and snarling in every direction! Chasing the sharks away!

Until at last, there wasn't a single shark left in sight...

...and the water around us went quiet.

Well almost quiet!

"**WILL!** *(shake)* **YOU!** *(shake)* **LET!** *(shake)* **ME!** *(shake)* **GOOOOO!**" yelled Blaze and with one last furious

> **FLICK** <

he tossed Sneagle from his tail.

And I think it was only **then** that he realised what he'd done.

"**Wait...**" he whispered, looking around, "Where are the ..? **Wait, did I..?**"

I nodded, beaming with pride as,

"**Woohoo!**" whooped the sea dragons and "**Amazing!**" they cheered and,

"BRAVO!" boomed Wharla, clapping Blaze on the back, "NOT BAD FOR A LAND DRAGON! YOU KNOW, IF YOU EVER FANCIED A JOB..."

"Oh, erm, thank you," said Blaze blushing until his blue cheeks went purple. "But I, er, already have a job. I have to get these kids to the Pirate King!"

"PIRATE KING, EH?" said Wharla thoughtfully. "AND DO YOU HAVE A GOLD COIN FOR THE PIRATE KING?"

"Well no," admitted Blaze. "Not yet."

Wharla smiled.

"THEN PERHAPS I CAN HELP," he said and he began to pat at his scales muttering.

"OF COURSE, WE SEA DRAGONS DON'T REALLY USE MONEY. BUT I DO LIKE TO KEEP THE ODD GOLD

COIN HANDY FOR SUPERMARKET TROLLEYS AND SUCH...AH-HA! HERE WE ARE!"

And from some hidden pocket in his glittering green scales, Wharla pulled a fat gold coin.

"Oh, thank you, Your Highness," gasped Blaze swimming forward and taking the coin. "Thank you very much indeed!

"NOT AT ALL!" said Wharla. "NOW LET'S GET YOU TO THAT PIRATE KING, SHALL WE?"

He turned to the other dragons.

"BUBBLE RING!" he boomed.

At this strange command, the sea dragons rushed to make a ring around us. Then they began to swim in a circle, **FASTER AND FASTER**, snorting streams of bubbles as they went.

At first it was like being trapped in the middle of a very dragon-y merry-go-round.

But as they **SPED UP** everything became a

80

blurry blizzard of bubbles until I couldn't see a thing!

"GET READY!" yelled Blaze over the noise of the bubbles and,

"READY FOR WHAAAAAT?" screamed Hannah.

And then there was a giant

POP!

The dragons were gone. The sea was gone. Even Sneagle was...nah, just kidding. Sneagle was still there. We were definitely stuck with him!

Our little gang was standing on the beach of what looked very much like a tropical island!

Everyone was dry, Blaze was back to toy size and for a second I thought things were **finally** going our way.

Until...

"MONSTER!" squeaked Blaze pointing up the beach.

And quick as a flash he buried himself under my arm, covering his eyes with his paws.

Which was understandable...

...but not really going to help.

CHAPTER TEN

Rushing towards us over the sand was an enormous octopus.

It was huge! As in, it would definitely have bumped it's head getting through a doorway. But on the plus side it was wearing a big smile...and an even bigger frilly apron!

"Welcome to the Island of the Pirate King!" said the octopus, in a very musical, posh-lady sort of voice. **"You must be here for the ice cream."**

"Ice cream?" squeaked Blaze, peeking out from between his paws in surprise and,

"Yes!" nodded Sneagle excitedly. "Ice cream! That's EXACTLY why we're here!"

"Sneagle!" said Hannah. "That's not..."

But the octopus wasn't listening.

"People said I should sell my ice cream from a yucky van," she told us. **"'Why not move around?' they said. But I said NO. My little ice cream shop is...SPECIAL. Just LOOK!"**

She pointed up the beach with her tentacles, and...

WOW!

In the shade of the palm trees was an ice cream shop. But this was no ordinary shop!

The roof looked like giant scoops of ice cream stacked on top of each other. There were waffle cone walls, a door made of chocolate flakes and two large windows edged with sweets and sprinkles.

"Is it made of real ice cream?" gasped Sneagle.

Yummy gave a tinkling, musical laugh.

"Oh, what an idea!" she said smiling at Sneagle. And then she turned to us saying, **"Isn't he sweet?'**

Blaze looked tempted to say 'NO'. But instead he said,

"It's just built and painted in clever ways to LOOK like ice cream, Sneagle! Don't go trying to eat the nice lady's shop!"

Sneagle looked unconvinced. We'd have to keep an eye on him.

Meanwhile Hannah was peering up at the sign above the door.

"YUMMY'S ICE CREAM PARLOUR," she read.

"I'm Yummy," explained the octopus. **"And I make all 372 flavours of ice cream myself using a secret recipe."**

She grinned around at us.

"So I hope you're hungry," she added.

"Starving!!" screeched Sneagle but,

"Sorry," said Hannah, grabbing one of Sneagle's legs as he flapped towards the shop. "But I'm afraid we don't have time for ice cream. We came to find the Pirate King!"

Yummy's face fell but then,

"Oh! I can help with that too!" she cried excitedly. **"I've got a treasure map that will lead you right to him. It's up at the shop. Come along!"**

She turned and set off up the beach and Sneagle tugged himself out of Hannah's grip to follow.

"Ice cream AND a tasty map to nibble!" he squawked. "Best day ever!"

But the rest of us didn't move.

"What do you think?" whispered Hannah.

"A map would be helpful!" admitted Blaze.

"I thought you knew where we

needed to go!" hissed Sugar crossly.

"I knew the way to the island," mumbled Blaze, looking a bit embarrassed. 'But now we're here...well...it's a bigger island than I expected and...well...finding the exact spot..."

"I'm sure you'd be able to find him Blaze!" said Hannah kindly. "But having a map as a back up plan can't hurt! Come on then!"

Blaze looked relieved and we set off after Yummy and Sneagle, who were already chatting away like old friends.

But as we all got closer to the shop Hannah started to frown. Then, without a word, she took my hand and gave it a squeeze.

Secret signal again!

But get ready for what? What could possibly be dangerous about an ice cream shop?

"In you go! That's it!" fussed Yummy as we got to the door and she ushered us all inside.

As I brushed past the door frame, a tiny bit of the wood broke off and it looked so realistic.

Just like ACTUAL REAL chocolate

flake!

"Like the gingerbread house in Hansel and Gretel," I thought, smiling to myself at the idea.

But if the outside of the shop reminded me of a fairy tale, that was NOTHING compared to the inside.

"Woah!" breathed Blaze looking round. "That's a LOT of pudding!"

Sneagle didn't say anything at all. He was clutching at his chest trying to breathe.

Behind the gleaming glass counter were hundreds of tubs of brightly coloured ice creams.

The walls were lined with shelf after shelf of sticky sauces and glass jars, holding every topping you could ever possibly imagine!

Go ahead! Imagine a topping right now...

YEP! That one was there!

"So what can I get for you?" smiled Yummy. **"Chocolate? Toffee? Or maybe just a little bit of everything?"**

"A bit of EVERYTHING?" squawked Sneagle his eyes wide. "Are you serious?"

But,

"Just the map, please," said Hannah in her fake cheerful voice.

"Oh, of course, of course!" beamed Yummy and she ducked under the counter.

Next to me Hannah tensed, ready for a trick or even a fight but,

"Here you are, Sweetie!" said Yummy and she popped back up holding out a yellowing treasure map.

"Oh!" said Hannah, trying to hide her surprise. "Erm...thanks!"

And I could tell she relaxed a lot as she took it. Especially when it didn't explode or anything!

"No problem, Sweetie!" smiled Yummy. **"Now are you SURE you won't have a quick ice cream**

before you go? Free of charge?"

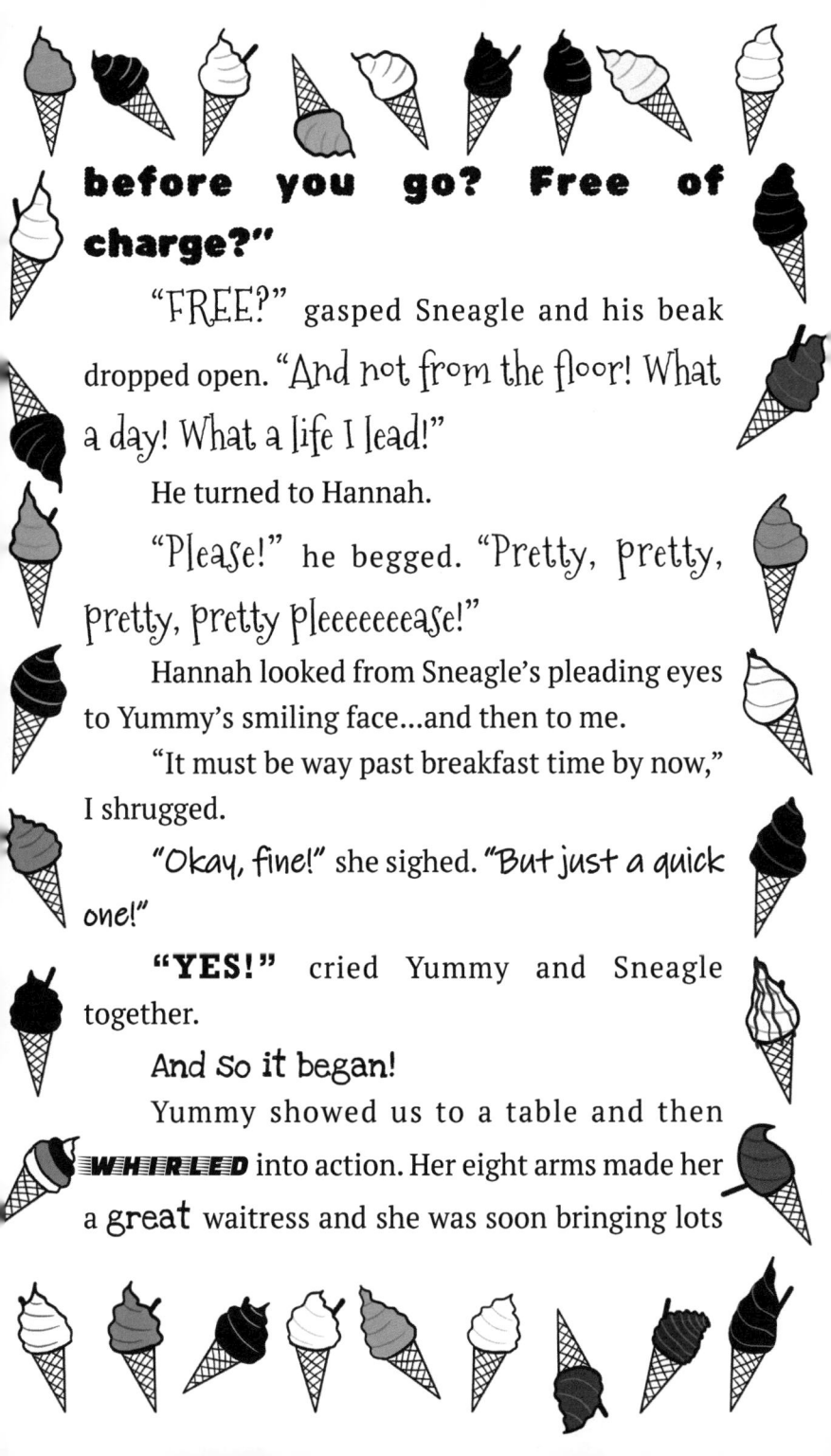

"FREE?" gasped Sneagle and his beak dropped open. "And not from the floor! What a day! What a life I lead!"

He turned to Hannah.

"Please!" he begged. "Pretty, pretty, pretty, pretty pleeeeeease!"

Hannah looked from Sneagle's pleading eyes to Yummy's smiling face...and then to me.

"It must be way past breakfast time by now," I shrugged.

"Okay, fine!" she sighed. "But just a quick one!"

"YES!" cried Yummy and Sneagle together.

And so it began!

Yummy showed us to a table and then **WHIRLED** into action. Her eight arms made her a great waitress and she was soon bringing lots of different flavours for us to try.

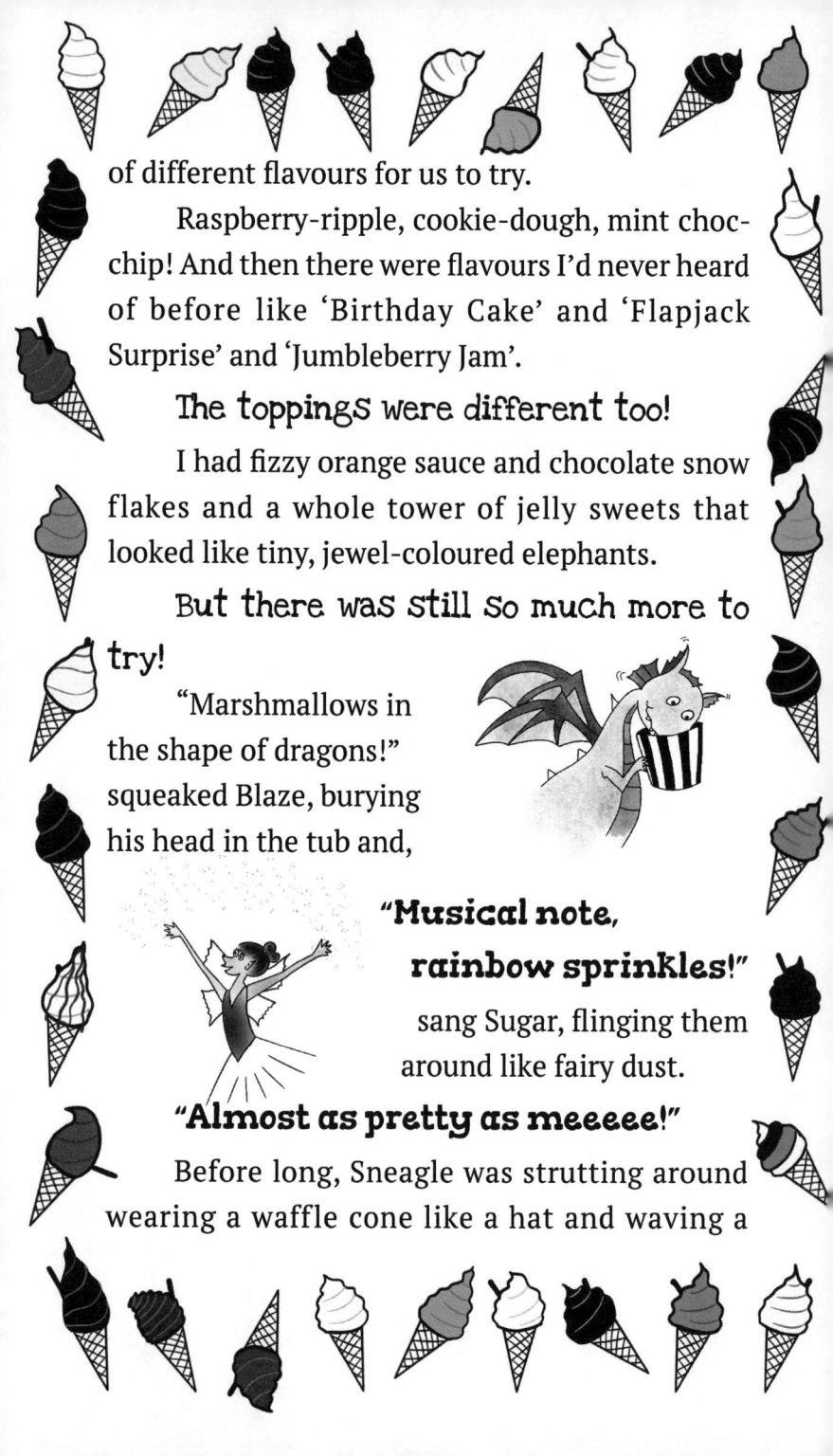

Raspberry-ripple, cookie-dough, mint choc-chip! And then there were flavours I'd never heard of before like 'Birthday Cake' and 'Flapjack Surprise' and 'Jumbleberry Jam'.

The toppings were different too!

I had fizzy orange sauce and chocolate snow flakes and a whole tower of jelly sweets that looked like tiny, jewel-coloured elephants.

But there was still so much more to try!

"Marshmallows in the shape of dragons!" squeaked Blaze, burying his head in the tub and,

"Musical note, rainbow sprinkles!"

sang Sugar, flinging them around like fairy dust.

"Almost as pretty as meeeee!"

Before long, Sneagle was strutting around wearing a waffle cone like a hat and waving a chocolate flake, saying he was a wizard.

It was hilarious!

Then Hannah suggested a competition to see who could build the highest tower of ice cream.

Everyone was having so much fun!

Yummy kept refilling our bowls with **more** and **more** and **more** and **more**. At some point we each moved to our own table so there'd be **more** room for **more** sauces and **more** sweets and **more** sprinkles and...

more...

and **more**...

and SNORE...

I don't remember falling asleep! But I remember the waking up bit! That bit was BAD!

CHAPTER ELEVEN

"Everyone! WAKE UP!" hissed Hannah. "You have to wake up RIGHT NOW!"

The thing was, I didn't want to wake up yet. I was having a lovely dream about ice cream.

"Five more minutes," I mumbled but,

"No! Now!" insisted Hannah and she started shaking at my shoulders. "Look outside! LOOK!"

With a deep sigh I forced my eyes to open.

But what I saw didn't make any sense.

Sugar, Blaze and Sneagle were all yawning

and rubbing their eyes. They were lifting their heads out of sticky pools of melted ice cream.

What was happening?

It took a moment for it to sink in...

We'd all fallen asleep in the shop!

I looked over to the window. There was the beach and the sea and...

"Hannah, is that a SUNSET?" I gasped, sitting up at once. "How long have we been asleep?"

"I think all day!" she grimaced, tugging me to my feet. "It's this shop! It's some sort of magical trap. We have to get out of here before..."

But at that moment the door swung open.

Yummy was back!

"Oh good, you're awake!" she smiled sweetly, sweeping back into the room. **"Would you like some more, more, MOOOOORE?"**

As she said it, the word **'MORE'** did a weird

kind of echo in my head.

Next to me, Sneagle and the toys began to nod, muttering **'MORE, MORE, MORE'**.

And I could feel my own head WANTING to nod and my own lips starting to ask for **MORE** but...

"No!" shouted Hannah, putting her hands over her ears and scowling. "We've finished! We're full! We've had..."

"STOP!" cried Yummy, and her eyes were suddenly wide with alarm. **"Don't say it! Don't say that wicked word!"**

"...enough!" finished Hannah grimly. And then, sensing she was on to something, she screamed it at the top of her lungs. "WE'VE HAD ENOOOOOUGH!"

Well that did it!

Yummy's panicking face twisted into full-on fury!

With an ear splitting roar, she lurched

towards us, tentacles grasping, screaming with rage!

"RARRRRRRRRRGH!"

But she couldn't reach us!

She was glued to the spot! Because down at the floor level, the rest of her body had started to **MELT.**

"**Whaa - aaaat?**" sang Sugar as she and the others snapped out of their trance. "**What's happeniiiiiiiiiiiing?**"

Good question! What was happening?

Yummy was still straining towards us, but her face was sinking lower and lower as her whole body melted into a **POOL OF CREAMY RAINBOW SLOP.**

"Errrrm, I think Yummy might have been a monster made out of ice cream!" I realised backing away.

"Oooooh! What flavour?" asked Sneagle peering forward.

"**Who caaaaaares!**" sang Sugar pulling him back by the wing. "**Let's just get out of here!**"

But THAT was easier said than done!

BECAUSE NOW THE WHOLE SHOP HAD STARTED TO MELT.

"It's not just Yummy!" gasped Hannah, as a huge chunk of ceiling slopped down right in front of us. "This whole place is made of ice cream! The walls! The roof! Everything!"

"Time to go!" squeaked Blaze but,

"Wait!" screamed Hannah. "The map!"

She **SLIPPED** past Yummy, whose apron was quickly becoming a frilly island in a sea of stickiness.

"NO! GLUG-GLUG,"

gurgled Yummy, as her furious face melted into the puddle. **"ENOUGH IS NEVER ENOUGH! YOU FOOLISH CHILDREN!!"**

Hannah snatched up the map and **RACED** back to join us. Then, together, we **BURST OUT** of the chocolate flake door and on to the beach.

And we were just in time!

There was an ear splitting

CRASH!

as the entire shop collapsed into a **SLOPPY, DRIPPING PILE OF MUSH.**

For a moment no one moved. We all just stared at the mess until...

"Normally I like naps!" squeaked Blaze, breaking the silence. "But that one was..."

He shuddered.

"It's sooooooooo late!" sang Sugar. **"And the flamingo attacks at midniiiight!"**

"We need to get to the Pirate King!" said

Hannah. "Like - NOW!"

She held up the map, twisting it this way and that and peering around the beach.

"It's that way!" she decided, pointing. "Not too far. Come on!"

And just like that she was off again, SPEEDING down the beach, with the rest of us PELTING after her.

But as we ran, I started to worry. Could we trust a map that came from Yummy? Or were we just running towards more trouble?

Before I could decide, something loomed out of the darkness ahead of us.

It was the crumbling wooden skeleton of an old pirate ship, laying wrecked on the sand.

Hannah gasped and we all stumbled to a stop in the ship's EXTREMELY spooky shadow.

Unfortunately for us, this shadow was being made by the moonlight. Because it was now FULLY dark!

We were running out of time.

"I don't understand!" said Hannah checking the map. "The Pirate King should be right here, in front of this shipwreck!"

"He IS here!" whispered Blaze. "I can feel the magic. But to meet a Pirate King you have to THINK like a PIRATE!"

Sugar rolled her eyes.

She doesn't like it when Blaze knows more about things than her. Especially magical things!

"Remember the gold coin we got from Wharla..?" Blaze said and he held it up to show us. "Well, REAL pirates bury gold coins so..."

"Yes, yes. Boring piratey stuff. Blah-de-blah!" sang Sugar. **"I'll do it!"**

And she **ZIPPED** through the air, snatching the coin from Blaze's paw as she went.

"Wait!" yelled Blaze.

But it was too late!

Sugar had landed next to the shipwreck and thrust the gold coin deep into the sand and...

Nothing happened!

"**Done!**" grinned Sugar, flying back to us. "**Now what?**"

It was as if the beach wanted to answer her question.

It gave a strange little quiver beneath our feet and above us the shipwreck creeeeeaked.

"Uh-oh!" gulped Blaze

The sand shivered again...

Another creeeeeeeeeeeeak from the boat!

"Sugar..." said Hannah slowly. "What did you do?"

"**Meeeee?**" sang Sugar. "**It was Blaze!**

It was his silly idea! He said..."

"But I hadn't finished!" snapped Blaze looking terrified. "And now you've gone and..."

But before Blaze could explain what Sugar had gone and done,

    the whole beach,

        the shipwreck,

            EVERYTHING went...

CHAPTER TWELVE

The shipwreck had vanished and in its place stood a magnificent sandcastle.

It was the kind of sandcastle you get from those **fancy** buckets. The ones with towers and turrets.

Only THIS sandcastle was the size of my school!

And standing in front of it was...

"**The Pirate King,**" breathed Sugar and she began ticking things off on her fingers with obvious delight. "**Long curly hair, dashing black hat, eye patch over**

one eye! D-reeeeeeeamy!"

But as Sugar went all *love-loopy* I noticed something. It **wasn't** actually an eye patch. It was just a stripey old sock on some elastic!

"**Oh my!**" sighed Sugar, fanning herself with her hand. **"He's soooooo handsome!"**

"Handsome?" sniggered Blaze. "The guy with the smelly old sock on his face?"

"I'm sure it's a clean sock!" snapped Sugar.

"But it's still a sock…" argued Blaze, as if Sugar was missing the point. "…on his face!"

"Is that the Pie Rat then?" asked Sneagle as the Pirate King began to swagger towards us. "I must say I was expecting a bit more pastry."

"Shush Sneagle!" hissed Sugar. **"You're messing up my** love-at-first-sight **moment!"**

But the Pirate King wasn't looking at Sugar. He was busy pointing a very sharp looking hook… at Blaze.

"*I'll be takin' your gold coin now!*" cried the

pirate. "*Hand it over, ya scurvy dog!*"

"Oh," gulped Blaze, trying his best to be brave. "I'm...erm...not a dog."

"And I'm afraid we don't have the coin any more," admitted Hannah, "because the beach sort of exploded."

Next to me, Blaze forgot to be scared and humphed.

"We WOULD have had a coin if Sugar had stayed out of it," he complained. "Because I knew what to do! You're supposed to put the coin in the sand BUT KEEP HOLDING IT!"

Sugar shrugged.

"Let's all just agree that Blaze's instructions were a bit rubbish and move on, shall we?" sang Sugar sweetly and she smiled at the Pirate King.

But the Pirate King did not smile back!

"*If you've no coin for me...*" growled the Pirate King. "*...then you'll be* **WALKING THE**

PLANK!"

"No! We ABSOLUTELY, DEFINITELY WON'T be doing that!" said Hannah cheerfully.

And I couldn't help smiling because the Pirate King looked both annoyed and a bit baffled about what to say next.

Hannah can have that affect on people.

"But about that whole 'WALK THE PLANK' thiiiiiing..." sang Sugar, trying to get his attention back to her. **"We reeeeeeeally need your help, Your Handsomeness!"**

"Yes!" nodded Hannah. "Because back at the beach there's this inflatable flamingo with a sparkly eye patch and..."

"*Wait!*" snapped the pirate, holding up his hook. "*What be the GEMS on this eye patch?*"

"Errr, I think they were blue and green," I said, trying to remember.

"*Emeralds and sapphires,*" he corrected with a far away, dreamy look on his face.

But then he scowled and stamped his foot.

"*That's MY eye-patch!*" he snarled. "*Darn and blast it!*"

And he began to stomp back and forth, muttering to himself.

"Well that explains the stinky sock on his face," whispered Blaze with a grin.

"**Clean sock!**" hissed back Sugar irritably. "**It's a clean sock!**"

Hannah gave them a warning look (that she definitely learned from our Mum) and they instantly zipped it.

"Excuse me, Mr Pirate King!" called Hannah and he paused in his stomping to squint at her. "But how did your eye patch end up miles away? And on an inflatable flamingo?"

"*Tis a strange tale!*" he whispered mysteriously. "*Y' see, I took it off to have a little nap, placed it on the sand beside me and when I woke up the tide had come in and PUFF! It was gone!"*

"**What a straaaaange and thrilling taaaaaale!**"

sang Sugar, fluttering her eyelashes, but Hannah looked far less impressed.

"So basically, you didn't look after your stuff and the sea washed it away," she said. "That's not exactly a mystery. That's just littering!"

"Well whatever you call it, it's been happening a lot lately!" I frowned, thinking back to the flamingo and her sand toy gang.

But the Pirate King wasn't listening!

"*Truth be told...*" he said, continuing with his story, "*...it be a magical eyepatch.*"

"We know!" said Hannah coldly, but the Pirate King kept going.

"*It makes people want to* **WALK THE PLANK!**" he chuckled.

"We know!" repeated Hannah, looking more and more cross by the second.

"And there's the whole 'bringing plastic to life' thiiiiing toooooo!" sang Sugar admiringly, **"He doesn't want to show off. So modest. Just like me!"**

"*What's that now? Bringing plastic to life, you say?*" frowned the Pirate King. But then his face split into a nasty grin. "*Why! That's new! An' that be very interestin' indeed!*"

"Errrm, it's actually causing a bit of a problem," I said, "Because..."

"*I want it BACK!*" snapped the pirate suddenly and he pointed his hook at Blaze.

"Return my magical eye patch, ye scurvy dog...or **WALK THE PLANK!**"

"I'm really, REALLY not a dog!" squeaked Blaze eyeing the spike of the hook nervously but determined to be...well, **NOT a dog!**

Meanwhile, Hannah had stepped between them looking equally determined!

"Give us something to defeat the inflatable flamingo," she said "and I promise I'll return your eyepatch myself!"

"Oh! No need for us all to come baaaack!" beamed Sugar. **"I can return the eye patch to this lovely gentleman. No trouble at aaaaaaall."**

Blaze rolled his eyes.

"An I'll keep you company if there's a reward!" chipped in Sneagle. "'specially if that reward is a doughnut!" he added hopefully. "I love doughnuts! Is the reward a doughnut?"

"No one mentioned a reward Sneagle!"

snapped Blaze. "The only reward is the sense of a job well done!"

"And no-one drowning!" pointed out Sugar.

"Well, yes! That too!" admitted Blaze, blushing.

The Pirate King squinted around our little group.

"To be sure, you're a motley crew of scurvy dogs..." he began.

"No dogs here!" muttered Blaze under his breath. "Literally not a single dog! Captain Sock-Face isn't a great listener, is he?

"But," shrugged the pirate. *"I suppose you nasty rapscallions have yourselves a deal!"*

"Mmmm! Sounds tasty!" grinned Sneagle. "Can you eat a rapscallion?"

"No ideeeeea!" sang Sugar. **"But what a lovely word! Rapscallion! Isn't this guy just a deliiiiiight!"**

Blaze rolled his eyes AGAIN and the Pirate

King began to rummage around in his long velvet coat until,

"*You'll be needin' THIS, me hearties!*" he grinned and he passed Hannah a white paper packet. She peered inside and...

"Fish and chips!" she said. Then she wrinkled her nose. "COLD fish and chips!"

"Did someone say COLD fish and chips?" cried Sneagle. "That is my favourite kind of fish and chips! Gimmee! Gimeee! Gimmee!"

At once he made a DIVE for the packet. But quick as a flash, the Pirate King snatched him out of the air.

115

"Greedy little thing, aren't you?" growled the pirate, frowning at Sneagle. "Well then, let me see..."

He bent his head down close to Sneagle and began to whisper something.

It was quite a long something! And poor Sneagle looked terrified!

Finally, our greedy little friend glanced between the chips and the pirate and,

"Okay!" he squawked with a little nod. "Understood!"

The Pirate King released him but Sneagle didn't dive for the fish and chips again.

Which was helpful, because we really needed to sort out this magical gift thing and get back!

"So the, er, COLD fish and chips...?" I prompted.

"...should put a stop to all the **WALK THE PLANK** magic, AYE!" nodded the Pirate King.

"And it's also a weapon because...CRABS!"

"Pardon?" said Hannah, frowning.

"Crabs!" he screamed pointing down the beach. *"It's those crabs from St Crabbles Primary School! And they're heading this way!"*

"Sugar, you've really hit the love jackpot this time!" grinned Blaze. "Sock on his face, thinks everyone's a dog and talks nonsense about crabs! What a guy!"

Sugar turned red, glaring at him.

But I wasn't sure it **WAS** nonsense. There was definitely something moving in the distance where he'd pointed. **And it did seem to be heading our way!**

Meanwhile, the Pirate King had flung himself onto the beach and was desperately trying to bury his own legs.

"What are you doing?" demanded Hannah. **"What's going on?"**

"They did a bake sale," spluttered the pirate. *"St Crabble's. To raise money for their*

library... And, well, I was hungry and crabs are surprisingly good at baking and well, truth be told, I might owe St Crabble's Primary a few gold coins...thousands actually so... Toodle-loo!"

"Toodle-loo?" gasped Hannah. "No! Wait! We're not done here!"

But the Pirate King was now throwing handfuls of sand at his feet.

"*Need a coin!*" he mumbled frantically, patting down his jacket. "*Need a... Aha!*"

And his face lit up as he whisked a gold coin from one of his pockets and shoved it into the beach.

Instantly, the beach around him gave a yucky, wet, **slurping** noise and sucked him down, down, down...right under the sand.

"Come back!" yelled Hannah. "How do the cold fish and chips become a weapon?"

But instead of an answer, the beach gave a rather rude

BUUUUUUUURP!

The Pirate King…was gone.

Unlike the 400 giant crabs from St Crabble's Primary. They weren't gone!

It turned out they were real! And heading right for us in an angry, churning mob!

CHAPTER THIRTEEN

"Tiiiiiime to goooooo!" sang Sugar and Hannah nodded.

Now you're probably thinking that we **DASHED** down to the sea and sailed home on Blaze the boat.

But that's not how it went!

Because as we started to run away from the crabs and towards the water, a **flash** lit up the sky followed by low rumble.

Thunder and lightning!

"That's it!" squeaked Blaze. "I don't care

120

if this IS a piratey seaside adventure. I'm not being a boat in a sea storm. I'll get water in my eyes! We're FLYING back home. No arguments!"

"Okay fine!" panted Hannah. "But let's hurry! We don't have time to fight those crabs. It must be nearly midnight by now!"

She was right! What if we were too late? What if Pirate Pink had already started sending children into the sea?

The thunder rumbled around us again and Blaze gave a little 'eeeek' of fright. Quickly, Sugar dusted him to make him grow and we all scrambled onto his back.

And then we were off, Blaze **BLASTING** into the sky **LIKE A ROCKET**.

Luckily it wasn't raining! But Blaze had to **SWOOP** and **SWERVE** as forks of lighting spiked through the sky around us.

He squeaked a few times, but he was very brave and VERY FAST!

It wasn't long before the beam of the lighthouse was sweeping around ahead of us. It was guiding us home!

Unfortunately, that's not all it was doing!

"Oh no!" cried Hannah, pointing. "We're too late! LOOK!"

The beach should have been empty at this time of night. But instead it was almost full.

Full of children!

And there wasn't a single adult in sight.

"They look like they're sleep walking!" wailed Blaze.

"Right into the seeeeea!" sang Sugar.

"Ruby!" gasped Hannah. "What if Ruby..."

It was too awful a thought to finish.

"Blaze," I cried. "Get us down there, fast!"

But Blaze had stopped in mid air. He was hovering like a helicopter, frozen in shock.

Because down on the beach...the children had suddenly frozen too.

Every single one of them had stopped. They were just standing there, fast asleep, pyjamas flapping like flags in the gusts of the stormy night.

"What's haaaappening?" sang Sugar. **"Whyyyy have they stopped?"**

"I bet I know!" said Hannah grimly. "Blaze, can you get us to the lighthouse? We need to see what Pirate Pink is doing!

"But without HER seeing US!" I added quickly.

He nodded and in no time at all we were landing silently on the lighthouse roof. Following Hannah's lead, we all shuffled to the edge and peered down at the balcony below.

The beam from the lighthouse was sweeping round and round just above the balcony making things dark then light, dark then light.

And there was Pirate Pink! But she was having a problem with her nasty plan.

"Just a bit higher!" she screeched.

She was still wearing the Pirate King's eyepatch and straining upwards, stretching her neck to the very limit. Surely, any second now the gems would be high enough to catch the light again. And once they did, the sleepwalking children would restart their walk into the sea.

We had to do something! AND FAST!

"It was working fine until you idiots fell over!" screamed Pirate Pink **"Everyone stand up STRAIGHT!"**

That's when I noticed the rest of the gang. They had made themselves into a tower underneath her. Pirate Pink was balancing on top of Bucket. Bucket was wobbling on top of Spade. And down at the bottom Spade was staggering about, trying to keep them all steady.

"**I'm so close!**" screamed Pirate Pink in frustration. "**Tiny, climb onto my head and help!**"

But Tiny the turtle was staring at the beach, her eyes wide with horror.

And then, very slowly, she shook her head.

"I tink I doesn't want to help," she whispered.

"**What!**" shrieked Pirate Pink.

Tiny turned to face the flamingo, looking pale.

"I tink we mustn't hurt d' ickle ones," she whispered bravely. "Dey are ony ickle. My Ruby left me... But I tink it was oh-nee a...a...acky-dent!"

Pirate Pink twisted her long neck to peer at Tiny.

"**I brought you to life,**" she snarled.

"And that means YOU DO WHAT I SAY! Now stop talking rubbish and get over here and HELP!"

Pirate Pink returned at once to her desperate stretching for the beam of light…but Tiny didn't move.

I held my breath, waiting to see what Tiny would do next. One second…two…and then…

"No," she said, so quietly that the wind almost carried it away.

But Pirate Pink had heard.

"NO?" she shrieked and she twisted to face Tiny so quickly that she sent Bucket and Spade clattering to the floor beneath her.

"Ouch!" mumbled Spade from somewhere underneath her.

Pirate Pink bounced from the pile towards Tiny.

Her voice was dangerously quiet as she loomed over the trembling toy.

"Your precious little Ruby doesn't love you any more," she whispered softly. '**She**

left you to ROT."

Tiny gave a little gulp as Pirate Pink leaned in even closer.

"Except plastic doesn't rot, does it Tiny? You'll still be floating around in the sea 500 years from now...all alone!"

Tiny's lip wobbled at this but Pirate Pink pressed on.

"And 500 years is a such long time to be all on your own, Tiny," she pointed out sadly. "So I want you to think very VERY carefully now... Are you part of this gang...or not?"

Tiny looked between Pirate Pink and the

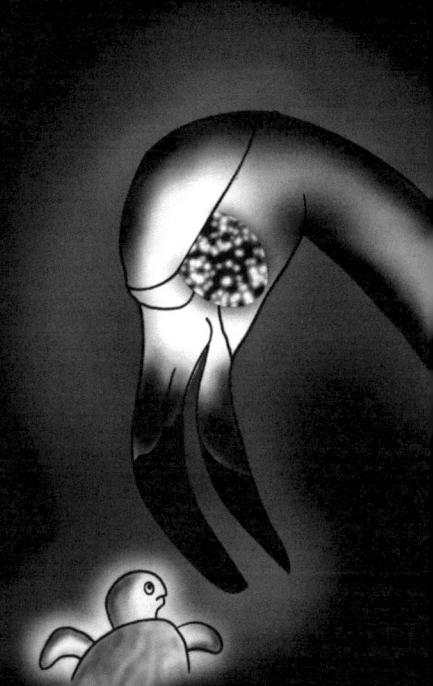

beach full of children. Her eyes were brimming with tears but...

"Not!" she squeaked and suddenly she was stamping her flipper. "Not! Not! NOT!"

Pirate Pink's patch free eye widened in surprise. But the shock quickly turned to rage.

"Then you really are just a useless bit of beach litter!" she spat.

And in one swift movement, she plucked Tiny up in her beak...

...and tossed her off the lighthouse tower!

129

CHAPTER FOURTEEN

Blaze **SWOOPED** to the rescue **SO FAST** that he was just a blue blur **WHIZZING** through the darkness!

He snatched Tiny from the air and **IN A FLASH** she was with us on the roof. (And in one of my sister's crushing hugs.)

"Don't worry!" whispered Hannah fiercely. "You're safe now!"

Meanwhile, Sugar was glowing so red with rage that we could have used HER as a lighthouse.

"**That Pirate Pink,**" she snarled,

clenching her fists, **"is an absolute BEAST!"**

"Did someone say FEAST?" asked Sneagle with a cheeky wink.

I think he meant it as a joke. To calm everything down a bit. But for Blaze, it was the last straw.

"No Sneagle!" he hissed. "No one said FEAST! Because in case you haven't noticed there's a beach full of tiny kids down there! **IN DANGER!**"

"Yes!" began Sneagle. "I can..."

But Blaze wasn't done!

"So unless you want to forget about your tummy for once and actually start **HELPING**," he whispered. "You should just...just...**go!**"

Sneagle's beak fell open in astonishment.

He looked at the kids on the beach. Then he looked at the rumbling thunder clouds up above. Finally he turned back to us.

For a second his eyes lingered on the fish and chips tucked under Hannah's arm.

And then,

"Fine!" he shrugged and he took off into the night sky.

But he didn't fly away!

He dived right at Hannah...and the fish and chips!

OH NO!

He was going to EAT our weapon!

Sneagle snatched the packet from under Hannah's arm and quickly flew out of reach. But then he did something really SHOCKING!

He **FLUNG** the packet with all his might, up into the stormy sky.

Up it went, higher and higher. But just when I thought it would drop back down...**it froze in** mid air!

And as it hovered in the sky, the wrappings of the packet began to open. Like the papery petals of a greasy flower.

And then...

SHAZAM!

A fork of lightning sliced down through the darkness. It hit the fish and chips and

SHWAR-ZING!

Suddenly a magical golden light was blazing in every direction, blasting out from the fish and chips.

It was as if someone had switched on

the sun in the middle of the night!

The magical daylight lit up the lighthouse. It lit up the sea. And then it lit up the beach!

And as the magical, fish-and-chip sunshine fell on the children...every single kid turned around. Then they began to gently float and fly through the air... AWAY FROM THE SEA!

I couldn't believe it!

They were all still fast asleep, but the magic was **WHIZZING** them back home!

Back to safety! Back to their cosy warm beds!

"TA-DA!" cried Sneagle looking smug. "HELPING! Just like Blaze and that RAT PIE guy said!"

"Like the Rat Pie said?" gasped Hannah. "Wait a minute! Sneagle! Did the Pirate King tell you what to do?"

Sneagle nodded.

"That's what he whispered when he grabbed you!" I realised, remembering. "He told you how to use the fish and chips to save all the kids!"

Sneagle nodded again.

"But how do the fish and chips become a weapon to defeat Pirate Pink?" asked Hannah. "So she can't do anything else?"

And that's when we heard the screaming from the balcony below.

"NOOOOOOOOOOOOOOO!"

Pirate Pink was staring at the beach in horror. **"How can this be?"** she gasped. **"WHAT..? WHEN..?"**

The glowing light from the fish and chips was fading now. But it had done its job!

The **WALK THE PLANK** magic from the eye patch had been completely destroyed.

The beach was empty!

"Who did this?" demanded Pirate Pink, coming to her senses, and next to me I felt Hannah brace for a fight.

But Pirate Pink didn't look up to where we were hiding on the roof. Instead she glared at the fish and chips floating above her.

"What IS that up there?" she screamed.

Sneagle winked at us. Then he flapped out to join the glowing food so that Pirate Pink could see him.

"ITS FISH AND CHIPS!" he yelled at the top of his lungs.

"FISH AND CHIIIIIPS!"

And then they came!

SEAGULLS.

Hundreds of them!

Until the whole sky was churning with birds.

"Wait!" cried Pirate Pink, nervously. **"Stop that! What are you doing?"**

"Just what that Rat Pie guy asked me to do!" called Sneagle happily.

And with a cheery wink, he booted the fish and chips down towards the lighthouse balcony...

where they scuffed to a stop...

...right in front of Pirate Pink!

"How DARE you kick things at me!" screamed Pirate Pink but Bucket and Spade were curious.

"What is it, Doris?" asked Spade.

"Is it a present?" asked Bucket excitedly. "Is it my Birthday?"

Pirate Pink didn't answer. She was glaring at Sneagle.

"Come down here RIGHT NOW!" she

demanded. **"Come down here and fight me, bird to bird!"**

Sneagle shook his head, grinning. Meanwhile Spade had started to poke at the packet.

"Oh, it's fish and chips!" he cried. **"That's nice! Doris, someone has sent us a take away!"**

But then he jerked back in disgust.

"Ergh!" he cried. **"It's COLD! Cold fish and chips! Yucky!"**

That's when it hit me!

COLD FISH AND CHIPS! If it was Sneagle's favourite food, it was probably EVERY seagull's favourite food.

"Cold fish and chips?" frowned Pirate Pink and,

"COLD FISH AND CHIPS!" screamed Sneagle.

He yelled it like it was a battle cry!

And then he dropped into a perfect dive,

SHOOTING towards the food on the balcony.

And Sneagle wasn't the only one after a tasty treat!

Above us the swirling cloud of seagulls burst into bits as every single bird went **RACING** down after Sneagle.

Suddenly the balcony below us was a flapping, squawking, mess of CHAOS!

And right in the middle of it all...

"ARGHGHG!" cried Pirate Pink. **"This isn't...in....the plan! I have...CHILDREN TO DROWN. STOP! NO! ARGHGHGHGHGH!"**

Bits of fish and chips were flying in every direction as the seagulls screamed in delight, fighting and snatching and pecking!

But then there was a much smaller noise, down by my feet.

"Ohhhh!" squeaked Tiny, swaying on the spot. "I feel a ickle bit...I tink I is maybe... Ohhhhh!"

Suddenly Tiny went stiff...**then she clattered to the floor!**

CHAPTER FIFTEEN

"Tiny what's happening? What's wrong?" asked Hannah, scooping the turtle up into her hands and looking around. "Somebody do something!"

But Tiny gave a small shake of her head.

"Just take me back to my Ruby!" she whispered. "I knowsies she never meanted to lose me. Take me back to my Ruby so she can play with me...and I'll be happy!"

Tiny gave a weak smile and then...she went still!

We all stared in silence at the toy cupped in Hannah's hands. We waited for it to move again…but it didn't. It was just a plastic sand toy.

Eventually Hannah said, "Ruby will be glad we found you!" and she gave the toy a little kiss before slipping it into her pocket.

"Hold on a minute!" sang Sugar. **"It was Pirate Pink that brought Tiny to life!"**

"So?" said Blaze, looking puzzled.

"So if Tiny has gone," sang Sugar, sparkling silver with excitement, **"maybe it's because Pirate Pink has gone too?"**

Quickly we all peered down to the balcony and sure enough…

The fish and chips had been gobbled up. The seagull mob had flown away. And Pirate Pink… Well…

She was jut a swim ring flamingo
THAT HAD BEEN POPPED!

"Crikey!" gasped Blaze. "Those greedy seagulls pecked her to bits!"

"Oh! That's dreadful!" said Hannah, sadly.

"But not WHOLLY undeserved,"

141

grinned Sugar. "**Get it? Wholly, like 'completely', but also 'HOLE-Y', because she's full of holes! It's a homophone joke!**"

"I feel like if you have to explain jokes, that's normally a bad sign," muttered Blaze.

Sugar stuck her tongue out at him.

"**What about Bucket and Spade?**" wondered Hannah.

Blaze swooped down to what was left of Pirate Pink. He lifted a floppy pink edge and there underneath were the other beach toys.

They were stiff and still...just like Tiny.

"**Pirate Pink popped and all her magic popped with her!**" sang Sugar.

"Yep!" agreed Blaze nodding. "The magic's definitely gone from these two!" He turned to Hannah. "Would Ruby like a bucket and spade to go with that turtle?"

"**I'm sure she'd love that,**" beamed Hannah.

"And that just leaves the eyyyyye patch," sang Sugar, swooping down to tug it from the Pirate Pink pile. **"I'd better go and return this to that lovely Pirate Kiiiiiiiiiing!"**

"We'll come too!" said Hannah, trying to hide a yawn behind her hand but,

"Oh no you won't!" said Blaze firmly. "I'm taking you kids home, right now! **It's time you were in bed!"**

Hannah was way too tired to argue, so Sugar zipped away and Blaze flew us home.

When we finally crept into bed, I could hear

Uncle Ed's noisy snores. **That was good!** It meant that the lifeguard and the ice cream man were probably safe somewhere too.

We were almost asleep when Hannah remembered the one thing that we'd all forgotten.

"Oh my goodness!" she gasped, sitting up in bed. **"Whatever happened to Sneagle?"**

Blaze twitched one eye open.

"Probably flew off to find more yucky bin food," he shrugged.

"That DOES sound like Sneagle!" I agreed with a sleepy grin.

"Okay," Hannah nodded and she lay back down. **"That makes sense."**

But as I fell asleep, something about that didn't quite make sense to me.

***

The next day was sunny and bright. Not 'magical-glowing-chips' sunny and bright. **Just the ordinary kind!**

Sugar had flown all night to return the eye patch to the Pirate King...

"He told me to go away or he'd feed me to the crabs," she told us, grinning. **"He's TOTALLY in love with me!"**

Anyway, on her way back she'd checked in on the lifeguard and the ice cream man.

Everything was back to normal.

We left the toys to have a nap and went to check on our family.

They were fine again too! Sort of...

"D'you know the best thing about holidays?" Mum was saying as we walked in.

"Yep," grinned Dad. **"I do. It's ice cream!"**

Hannah giggled and Mum answered her own question, ignoring him.

"It's that the days just drift by," smiled Mum happily. "And you can't really remember what you've done."

"Yep!" nodded Uncle Ed. "Like yesterday. I know I had a good long swim in the morning, but the rest of the day is a complete blur."

"Same here," shrugged Dad happily. "I don't remember a single thing after breakfast time yesterday!"

"Me neither," agreed Mum and for a second she looked thoughtful about that. But then she shrugged and smiled again. **"We must be SO relaxed!"**

Hannah and I shared a secret smile.

I had no idea how the magic worked when we went on adventures. But as long as we weren't in any trouble with Mum and Dad, I was happy!

"Oh, and by the way kids!" said Uncle Ed. "I found you something on the beach this morning... when I went for my run! He was by the bin. And he's a bit broken so I think he needs a new home."

He popped out of the room and when he came back he was holding a kite. Hannah took it and gasped.

"Look!" she whispered to me, tapping the picture on the kite. "It's Sneagle!"

Because that's who it was!

The seagull picture on the kite had the same hungry expression and the same happy grin.

I couldn't believe it!

All that time Sneagle had been just another toy, brought to life by the magic...and we had never suspected!

"I'm glad you picked him up, Uncle Ed," smiled Hannah, "before he got blown away, or washed out to sea and totally lost."

"Lost!" echoed Ruby sadly, looking up from her game. "Ruby lost her turta!"

"Oh, I almost forgot!" laughed Hannah and she dashed off to fetch Tiny.

When she got back Ruby squealed with delight.

"TURTA!" she cried and she hugged Tiny tight to her chest. "Ruby loves her turta!"

"And we found these too!" Hannah added, passing her the bucket and spade.

Ruby hugged them tight, then dropped to the carpet to pretend she was playing in the sand.

"So what shall we have for dinner tonight?"

asked Mum.

"Ice creams?" grinned Dad.

Hannah giggled.

"Or," said Dad getting excited. **"Ice creams squished into the shape of fish and chips!** That would be the perfect sea-side dinner. Where can we buy that?"

"Or just normal fish and chips!" suggested Uncle Ed quickly. "But let's eat them inside! Those cheeky seagulls already ate our ice creams. They can't have our chips too!"

"And seagulls do LOVE fish and chips!" nodded Mum.

"They REALLY do!" agreed Hannah, giving me a secret wink.

And that night as I scoffed my fish and chips (sneaking the odd chip to Blaze of course) it was easy to see why!

Fish and chips ARE delicious...

...but I wouldn't eat them cold!

Who would you draw fighting sharks?

How do you make an octopus laugh?

Give them TEN TICKLES!

Quiz: Which character are you?

1. You wake up and it's a bad hair day. Do you:
a) Not worry, crazy hair will be all the better for scaring off sharks.
b) Hide it under your hat and make anyone who mentions it walk the plank.
c) Cover your head in ketchup and eat your own hair. And your hairbrush.

2. Disaster! You've don't have your PE kit. Do you:
a) Search for the evil shark that stole your PE kit.
b) Start digging up the classroom floor - you'll have buried a spare kit somewhere.
c) Eat everyone else's PE kit.

3. Your teacher asks you to tidy the book area. Do you:
a) Search for dragon pictures shouting, "Fear not noble dragons, I shall rescue you from your paper prison!"
b) Call your teacher a scurvy dog and run out to

play.

c) Cover all the books in custard and eat them.

4. You're at the school fair when you spot the cake stall. Do you:

a) Go to buy a cake, then remember you gave your last gold coin to a land dragon to help him on his quest.

b) Eat every cake and then run away without paying.

c) Suggest that next time they add some cold fish and chips to the cakes for extra flavour. And then try to eat them all anyway.

If you've answered mostly A, you're Wharla. Mostly B, you're the Pirate King. Mostly C, you're Sneagle.

E	K	G	E	C	O	Q	T	P	M	T	P	G	E
C	U	A	L	I	G	H	T	H	O	U	S	E	Y
O	C	S	D	C	M	T	W	H	A	R	L	A	E
I	H	C	O	E	A	I	D	H	M	B	R	Z	P
O	I	U	B	C	P	N	W	K	I	C	X	J	A
V	P	K	S	R	J	Y	W	U	K	G	U	O	T
M	S	Y	H	E	W	Y	U	M	M	Y	R	G	C
B	S	T	T	A	P	I	R	A	T	E	M	L	H
N	U	N	U	M	Q	X	S	E	J	S	S	G	K
I	B	C	E	Q	M	V	U	S	J	C	K	Q	N
T	I	M	K	A	C	I	L	P	G	N	O	A	B
D	K	R	R	E	G	S	H	A	R	K	S	Y	Y
Y	A	X	Q	B	T	L	M	D	F	K	F	G	L
O	Q	Z	R	K	I	Y	E	E	A	S	Y	U	V

SPADE

BUCKET

WHARLA

SNEAGLE

YUMMY

SHARKS

ICE CREAM

PIRATE

LIGHTHOUSE

TINY

EYE PATCH

CHIPS

Go to www.jennyyork.com for lots more FUN!